Creative Patterns 1

Coloring Books For Adults Vol.1

Karim Benyagoub

ISBN-10: 1507820933

ISBN-13: 978-1507820933

www.ingramcontent.com/pod-product-compliance
Lightning Source LLC
Chambersburg PA
CBHW080339290526
45790CB00010B/3761
9781507820933